"This is THE book to help parents stop parenting on autopilot. There are no shortcuts to the realisations needed for a better relationship with oneself and one's kids. It's an inside job."

Antonio Neves,** bestselling author of **Stop Living on Autopilot

"Rhythmic vignettes that draw on great wisdom. There are stanzas that you will want to frame and those that will keep running through your head. The advice is invaluable throughout."

Paul Dix,** behaviour expert and bestselling author of **When the Adults Change, Everything Changes

"Mel's wisdom couplets never fail to bring a smile to my face and fresh insights tickling my brain. What a brilliant way to convey such essential truths, in a form instantly accessible to anyone from ages one to 100!"

John David Mann,** co-author of the global bestselling classic, **The Go-Giver

"I'm always so very impressed with Mel; both with her work and, just as importantly...with her heart!"

Bob Burg,** co-author of the global bestselling classic, **The Go-Giver

MEL SCHMITZ

I Fed My Kid *to a* Bird *of* Prey

Poems for overwhelmed parents

clarity

I Fed My Kid to a Bird of Prey
Poems for overwhelmed parents

Clarity Publishing Sdn. Bhd.,
51-21-A Menara BHL Bank,
Jalan Sultan Ahmad Shah,
10500 Penang, Malaysia.

www.clarity8.com

1 3 5 7 8 6 4 2

Published by Clarity Publishing 2025

Cataloguing-in-Publication Data

Perpustakaan Negara Malaysia

A catalogue record for this book is available from the National Library of Malaysia

ISBN 978-629-98122-7-2

Printed in Germany

For Liam & Sophie

ABOUT THE AUTHOR

As a mother of two and educational psychologist with over two decades in the field, Mel Schmitz has earned her stripes navigating the precarious tightrope of parenting – from accidental bird-of-prey encounters (with the best of intentions, naturally) to discovering parenting's uncanny 'soul mirror' qualities: reflecting back parts of ourselves we hadn't bargained for.

Her other qualifications include surviving chronic sleep deprivation, mediating daily negotiations with tiny dictator-fashionistas and tech junkies, and maintaining some semblance of sanity while juggling career ambitions, partnership and parenthood.

In her professional life, Mel's had the privilege of supporting countless parents through their own journeys of triumph and terror. While neuroscience and child development theory have deeply informed her approach, becoming a mother herself revealed a profound truth: the journey of parenting is as much about our own growth and self-reflection as it is about raising our children.

These poems, born from equal parts love, exhaustion, and enlightening moments of self-discovery, are her parenting solidarity manifesto to every parent who's ever wondered if they're doing it right (spoiler alert: you probably are).

CONTENTS

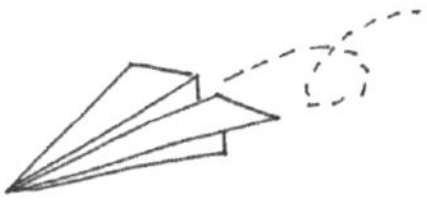

Introduction: A Little Note from Me

In my line of work
as a psychologist for kids,
I've listened to many wise souls,
If there's ONE thing I've learned
dear reader it's this:
Parenting's like a stroll on hot coals!*

I once thought I knew
Quite a lot 'bout this stuff,
(I'd read tomes on the topic, you see)
Then I became a new parent
(and my kid called my bluff)
I was forced to discover a new me.

I was sooo not prepared
for the existential trust,
I'd have to place in myself on this road,
But I've learned things since then,
and share them I must,
So I write this to lighten your load:

I hope that this book
will help you feel seen,
Make you giggle or just laugh out loud,
Question long-held ideas,
Inspire you to dream,
And find instances where you are proud-

Of the tricky task
you're somehow managing
(Even on days you feel like a jerk)
For the truth of the matter
is this simple thing:
Parenting's 'bout serious SELF-WORK!

From a fellow imperfect parent,
With much love,

mel♥

**Firewalking is the act of walking barefoot on hot embers or coals, an art form that stretches back across millennia and cultures. In order to do it without hurting oneself, pace is crucial: too slow, you'll burn yourself, too fast, and the risk of your feet sinking in ash increases… and you'll burn yourself too. It's a balancing act involving plenty of self awareness, mastery, discipline, faith and guts!*

EVERYDAY STRUGGLES

Lifeboats

Those days of 'hot and heavy'
Seem oh, so long ago!
Where lingerie was once strewn,
Now a baby radio…
There's a boob war that's going on,
(The clear winner is a baby
Who poops and squeals and never sleeps)
So maybe, oh just maybe…
We have to find a whole new way
Of exploring intimacy with each other
When we're not cleaning up the umpteenth poop,
Or pacifying jealous big brother.

When will I manage a shower?
Can I possibly sneak in a nap?
(How on earth does ol' Instagram
make this look like a natural snap?)
See no one ever warned me,
That I'd feel like such a lump,
(And that the highlight of my week
Would be baby managing a dump!)
My rainforest legs have forgotten,
the feel of a sharp razor blade,
And the very last thing I'm thinking of
Is the fun of getting laid!

What's happening? This is crazy!?!
I loved it once, 'twas totally fun-
Am I getting old? (Or simply lazy?)
I'm exhausted when the day is done!
Then I look over at haggard new dad-
And I know he's thinking it too,
We have to rearrange some time just for us,
To 'rediscover'the original crew!
See, we set out together on this journey,
(Some days I struggle to keep afloat)
But as I look at the tired face beside me,
I realise: We are each other's life boat!

Clothes Wars

In the toddler years:
'I DON'T want to wear a jacket, mama....
I'm really not cold outside!'
I look wearily at my petulant child:
(Arms folded, jaw set, legs wide)

How many times would we be destined
To repeat this nerve-fraying dance?
Would it take a bout of pneumonia
Before coats and hats got a chance?

Primary school time:
'No one CARES what I wear mama...
I'm telling you, this is perfectly fine'
I stare open-mouthed at my hard-headed kid:
Is she crazy? Does she think we're all blind?

Is wearing a favourite sweater,
Every day for a whole long week
What all the other kids do?
(Gosh that classroom must really reek...)

Teenage years:
'It's my body, I'll wear what I please mama...
It is MY freedom of expression'
I gaze at my pimply teen and think
'Guess the peer-pressure court is in session...'

What on earth will I do with her
If the hemlines get any shorter?
How will I explain my justified fears
To an unyielding teenage daughter?

As an adult:
Are YOU seriously going out in that mama?
Perhaps wear something more your age?
I stare at my kid, my eyes gleaming,
'But darling, this outfit's the rage...'

Just wait till you have some kids of your own,
Then you can tell THEM how to dress-
Now please excuse me, I need my phone
And my VPL* is a mess...

*Visible panty line. IYKYK

Z Zzz

Slumber Time Rhyme

C'mon, sleep!
Count those sheep!
Close those cute little eyes and slumber-

Please take a nap!
Just be a good chap,
The pounding in my head's like thunder!

Dear child close your eyes!
There's a lovely surprise,
For you in the land of sweet dreams-

Oh, why TF won't you sleep?
How on earth can you keep
Awake, making SUCH damn loud screams?

I don't know if you know:
You need rest so you grow
So come child, do us both a big favour:

Little baby, have some nods,
I'll be thanking all the Gods…
And you'll be waking to a parent you can savour!

Missing Teeth Parenting Fail

He looked at me in a mess,
blood oozing from his mouth,
I stared at his missing teeth
(my stomach going south),
This could not be happening!
My body frozen still
Numb from shock for the help I needed
desperately, until-

Parent instinct caught up-
I jumped back into gear,
Knowing that now, of all times,
was not the one for fear!
My husband cradled our crying kid,
while I rushed on to dial
Every number of my dentist friends
(which luckily I'd filed)

We lucked out, and one of them,
told us about a place-
That handled such emergencies,
Oh what a saving grace!
As my husband drove off with our kid,
(at super Grand Prix speed,)
I comforted my other child,
who like me, was in need-

Of a time machine to reverse,
that terrible event,
The fall, the crack, the missing teeth,
our minds completely spent...
The phone rang, it was a call
(and excellent advice)
'Don't forget to take the knocked out teeth,
did you apply some ice?'

I nodded but registered
that whilst we'd done the one,
The bits of chipped teeth were out there still,

on a pavement in the sun!
My daughter and I rushed out,
on our gruesome 'treasure hunt'
Wracked by guilt at the thought
that my son might bear the brunt-

Of my utter lack of common sense
and ability to think straight
(It's tough when one is panicking,
dear reader, can you relate?)
Glittering on the cement,
two bits of what we'd need-
I grabbed them and off I went
at super lightning speed!

His teeth got fixed, (but when he's 18
he'll definitely be 'crowned')
And the lesson that I learnt that day
is that when the chips are down
Somehow, someway, the strength I need
is already within,
(Even when my kid's a mess
and blood's flowing down his chin)

This parenting job is tricky,
some days I think I fail-
But these thoughts should never, ever
cause me to derail
My knowledge of the reality,
what I'll always know is true:
The kids are my greatest blessing-
Is that how it is for you?

Note: Every time I think deeply about this, I realise the kids are teaching me more about 'humaning' (verb: the business of being human) than I might actually be 'teaching' them.

Praise vs. Appreciation

Our kids need our appreciation
(It's a misnomer that what 'helps' is praise)
Only one's relevant in the creation
Of self-esteem in the children we raise.

Praise is pre-packaged approval
That comes from an external source
(and sometimes used like 'stain removal'
for mess-ups we've created by force)

Appreciation is a different creature-
'You are needed, Your value is seen'
A critical, growth-inspiring feature
Relevant to toddler, kid, adult or teen

So when we find ourselves flailing,
producing meaningless 'praising' soundbytes-
Appreciation will help smoother sailing
And be invaluable in setting things right.

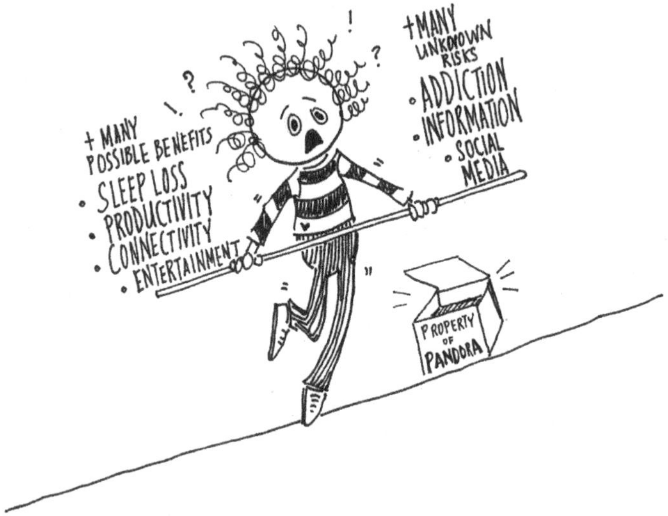
+ MANY POSSIBLE BENEFITS
• SLEEP LOSS
• PRODUCTIVITY
• CONNECTIVITY
• ENTERTAINMENT
+ MANY UNKNOWN RISKS
• ADDICTION
• INFORMATION
• SOCIAL MEDIA
PROPERTY OF PANDORA

Tech Tightrope Walk

Managing tech and kids is a tightrope walk,
'Balance' can feel impossible some days
Schools are no longer books, blackboards and chalk
Tech's in our lives in ubiquitous ways!

Sometimes I wonder if it's all so bad-
(There are moments I'm thankful for peace)
But is this changing my kid's brain? Why is he so mad?
If I suggest 'stop/eat/shower, please?'

I've read a bunch of terrifying studies
About the perils of tech addiction,
I don't want my kid to be an outcast with buddies,
But what IF this is a lifelong affliction?

So much of this stuff, is so very new,
No long-term studies to help on my way,
Social engagements online (I don't have a clue
How can I guide my kid with what to say?)

I've more questions than answers, impossible it seems,
What if something he posts online today,
Comes back to haunt him? (these unfathomable screens
Could mess up lives in a real, lasting way!)

And then I think of the many, many good things
that this tech has allowed us to enjoy
Video chats with loved ones, words with virtual wings
Guess I'll need to have faith in my boy!

For I cannot protect him in this changing space,
I must trust that I've raised him to know 'right'
To know his boundaries and values and grant him some grace,
Tech's a reality us parents can't fight.

Instead we should think through a different lens,
How do we teach discernment, moderation, grit?
Many a kid will want to play online with their friends
They need alternatives to this dopamine hit!

A
B
C

Material Matters

One doesn't really need a baby bathtub,
(That's what bathroom sinks are for)
And that fancy diaper station?
One soon learns that a bed or the floor
Offers similar functional features,
That get the job done just as well
For one's precious little creatures
Those early purchases are hell!

Buying baby's very first 'carriage'
('s harder than deciding on a car)
In fact, I tell you, many a marriage,
Involved less contemplation by far-
And what about baby's dwelling?
That Pinterest-worthy bedroom?
No way one wants to risk telling
A new parent 'bout the prospect of doom-

That soon their immaculate home will look,
Like a hurricane blew right through,
But who wants to be that 'reality crook'?
They'll know by baby #2!

Phone-y Baloney

I've something HUGE I must confess,
A white elephant in the room I must address,
And it's tough, because, I know it is true,
So I decided I'd unburden my failing to you.

Most days too much is happening 'round me,
I struggle with the to-dos, (though I try to break free),
I strive to create some structure in it all,
So my life doesn't feel like a constant free fall...

But this list, you see, it lives in my phone,
Which is the topic of this confessional moan,
The thing I sought as an aid, a smart fix,
Is the very thing that complicates the whole mix!

My phone, I've found, is a double edged knife,
It can detract as well as enrich my life,
I've made a pact with myself to more mindfully,
Navigate the art of this technology:

To do this I've written myself a 'lil song,
(Which I plan to set to music when the right tune comes along)
But I thought I'd share the lyrics with you,
In case it's a battle that you're fighting too:

'I know that screen is calling for you,
That blinking drug that pings and toots,
The likes, the comments, the swipes, the touch,
But when it all just gets too much-

Unplug that phone, get off that grid,
The time's limited you've got with your kid,
Soon they'll be on an independent roll,
And THEN you'll have all the time to scroll!

Till then remember to open your eyes,
The most important ones are those real lives,
You've been blessed to have within your four walls,
Be mindful of the time you spend on your calls!

All of us have the same hours to spend,
And the world is vast, but in the end,
When you're lying there, at the end of life's race,
You'll be with those for whom you've made space.

I know you want these faces to include your kids,
So resist doom scrolling or glomming on vids,
Till after they're in school or tucked up in bed,
Ignore that 'I'll just check' voice in your head...

You can really do this, they're watching you,
Don't wanna raise a generation of zombies anew,
Stuck to their screens like druggies on crack,'
That's it! Today I wrest my life back....

Toilet Spectators

I have an 'audience' who
Absolutely enjoy trips to the loo-

Trouble is, these days
Privacy is a haze-

A distant memory of the time
I could flush and recline...

Now I have to entertain
And somehow refrain

From yelling 'Get out of the loo
I need peace for a poo!!'

Kids are Expensive

To say "Kids are expensive"'s
An understatement at best,
No one tells you beforehand
Just how financially stressed
Many a hapless parent is,
By the stuff that we're told
Our newborns will TOTALLY need
Before they're a year old!

Then come the toddler years
And all of those toys
We feel we must purchase
To witness the joys
Of our little offspring
As they chortle with glee,
While we silently wonder
'bout that credit card fee...

One blink later,
the kids are off to school
A whole new set of purchases,
so they can feel 'cool'-
But hold on to your socks,
negotiations have just begun:
Those pocket money/allowance talks
are years from being done...

And then before you know it
Your acne-covered teen
Needs the latest tech and designer rags
So they can be seen
But if you think the shock's too great
From the cost of designer shoes,
Well, well my dear fellow parent,
I'm afraid I have sobering news...

For I have heard from others
Who are currently paying the price
And they assure me that college fees
Are anything but nice!

This parenting business means expensive years,
In more ways than might be apparent-
For we pay with money, our patience and tears,
Oh, the joys of being a parent!

Free Gift!

Boredom is deeply necessary,
it's not neglectful at all,
But fearing that it might seem so
leads some parents to fall
for the trap of constantly entertaining
Their offspring, oh-so-dear;
(Cause the thought of being 'negligent'
is something we all fear)
Unfortunately for these little
developing young brains
Healthy doses of boredom's needed,
because it truly trains
Resilience, lateral thinking,
Creativity that can't be taught
Dear parents give your kids some boredom –
the best present you never bought!

Parenting = Self-Work

A central truth about this parenting shtick,
Is that it's primarily about self-work,
Listen close, dear reader, this ain't no trick,
(But a reality some unknowingly shirk)

We've all read many a parenting book
Looking for hacks to make things go 'click'
Or a manual which somehow, by hook or by crook,
Makes a lesson we're trying to teach stick

This business is part self-confronting act,
Like looking in a soul-mirror of some kind,
We'd all like to ignore aspects of ourselves,
But damn, those kids manage to remind-

Us of those bits deep within our being,
That we'd rather keep oh-so-well hidden,
(Impossible of course when one is seeing
Those same things in our kids, unbidden!)

One cannot ignore the truth of the matter,
Parenting's about profound self work,
Gotta reach on inside, reconcile inner chatter,
Learn to recognise one's subliminal jerk-

A thoughtful question is one way
One can begin on this noble quest,
('cos questions can be most helpfully 'sticky'
They hang around in one's mind best...)

So dear parent, I hope as you do read
these silly little rhymes of mine,
perhaps, maybe, you'll feel the need,
(and somehow find the time)
To ponder on the questions
That spring up personally to you,
You're doing a great job-
this is ONE tough climb,
Remember: to yourself be true!

Definition: Self-work to me, is about continually reflecting on one's personal inner conversation/journey and striving to learn and improve one's self awareness and understanding of the role one plays in the lives of others.

SELF-COMPASSION

Anti-Martyr Anthem

For too long we've been sold a dumb story,
How it's persisted's beyond reason or rhyme,
Parenting's not about martyrdom glory,
(One learns this on the parenting climb!)

Of course in those earliest parenting years,
Many a hobby must rest on a shelf,
But there's more to life than poops, naps and tears,
Gotta remember to look after oneself!

Dear parent, listen closely, whatever you do,
Don't buy into ideas of perfection-
None of us are infallible (not a goal to strive to),
We're all humans in need of connection

And whatever it is you've been conditioned to think,
About self-sacrificing, martyr parent roles,
Just know that it's toxic (take the word of a shrink)
Martyr parents are NOT #parentgoals!

How might we become more mindful about observing and learning things from the parents around us whom we admire? Might this help us in rewriting our own ideas of what we think parenting should 'look like'?

HELP

Baby Blues Clues

Help! I'm feeling really blue,
'S not how I thought it'd be!
Baby's adorable, all wrinkly and new,
But I feel far from free:

My thoughts are spiralling around,
In a pit, a dark abyss,
Is THIS the supposedly profound
New mothering baby bliss?

I dare not utter these words aloud,
For fear it makes them more true,
Already a failure, can't cope with a crowd,
(Oh what the sweet f*#k should I do?)

Everyone is oohing and cooing,
And telling me how fast time'll fly,
But I don't have a clue what I'm doing,
And there are times I wish I could die…

Then the other day I met this mum,
Who took just one look at me-
Saw past unwashed hair, post-partum tum,
And said "Mama, it's YOU I see….

Baby blues, post-partum depression,
This beast has many a name,
Exhaustion, hormones, gene expression,
Lots can happen with this life change-

There's no shame in this experience you're braving,
Hang on Mama, there's help out there-
Put your mask on first, you're worth saving!
To do this job you first need air!"

CAUTION
UNDER CONSTRUCTION
HOT MESS
EXPECTATIONS
NEEDS
Passions
DREAMS
ReaLity

Hot-Mess Parenting

Have you ever felt like you're a hot mess?
Parenting's overwhelming but you're scared to confess-
That really some days you want to curl up and cry,
Or rock in a corner sobbing 'Why? Bloody, why?!?'

The dentist check-ups have been accidentally missed-
And you get the feeling that your kid's teacher is pissed:
You've forgotten some forms, mixed up meeting dates;
You're sinking in appointments that everyone hates…

You've got birthday treats to prepare for school;
But you're busy feeling like the ultimate fool-
Because you've just realised you almost forgot
The early pick-up time for your youngest tot…

Then ta-da! Your mobile phone rings,
(It's another kid, who forgot their sports things…)
You grab the nearest bag as you head out the door,
On your way to kindergarten, gas pedal to floor-

After which you arrive to deliver as requested:
The things your kid asked for, but alas, you've been bested …
Because your home organisation is totally shit-
You've accidentally grabbed the WRONG damn sports kit!

Are you shaking your head, do you know 'bout these days?
On this parenting journey you can mess up in ways
That you never thought would happen to you-
Don't worry there are millions of us doing this too!

Feelings

All feelings are valid;
All feelings allowed,
(Even the icky, messy ones,
of which we are not proud),
They all serve a purpose:
It's important to relate,
'Cos embracing ALL our feelings is
a panacea to self-hate!

No one needs the crushing pressure
Of being happy all the time,
Sometimes we're green with envy,
Sometimes pissed out of our mind!
Sometimes we feel so, so down,
we wonder if we'll survive,
Accepting and communicating our feels
is an important way to thrive!

We must be mindful of this fact,
in our daily reality,
And teach our kids that ALL feelings
deserve their fealty,
How else will they learn to like
their true authentic selves,
If they think that their unpleasant feels
must be banished to subconscious shelves?

But not all feelings should be acted on
(Some are best explained in words)-
A distinction to teach our daughter or son
So they find helpful ways to be heard.

No Blame Game

Self-compassion's enemy
has an odious name,
Darkly toxic and insidious,
we know him as 'Self-Blame'

He shows up unhelpfully at times
when we're our most distressed
Rejoicing in all of the things
We've simply gotten messed

But really he is just a big ol'
Toxic waste of space,
And we are all MUCH better off
if we show ourselves some grace.

"But HOW does one do this?"
I hear your exasperated ask-
"This doesn't sound like a simple
or easy-to-manage task!"

Tis' true, Self-Blame sings
One helluva catchy song,
But we can all learn how to
mindfully NOT play along-

By being intentionally conscious of
Our love-filled parenting WINS
We can find the counterpoint to
(Some of) our parenting sins

And something incredible happens
when we start to do this you see:
We BECOME the kind of parents
we've always wanted to be!

How can we become more mindful when these feelings of parental self-blame and guilt crop up?

Let's do a little experiment: Let's write a list of things that we've managed to do as a parent that we are proud of. It could include ANYTHING, no victory is too small. Have we managed to get our kid to dress without screaming? Great! Managed to get our teen to talk to us about something that did not involve asking for money? Score! Not exploded at a difficult power-struggle moment? Gosh, we rock!

"CHILD CARE
SELF CARE"

Be Aware: Practice Self-Care!

An unpredictable adult-
Can be downright scary;
We've all had those moments,
When our own kids are wary
Of our reactions,
the crap that we might say;
When we're sleep deprived, stressed
Or haven't eaten all day

That's why self-care's an all-important tool,
It gives us the greatest hope of keeping our cool
We all owe our kids this 'service' at least:
(Our best chance at managing that freak inner beast)

So take time, eat/sleep/exercise without guilt:
Parenting nirvana was never built
On the foundations of begrudged martyrdom stress
We must look after ourselves to parent our best.

Animal Sacrifice

I once fed my kid to a bird of prey;
('Twas not what I set out to do that day)
But sit back and hear the sorry tale,
If you're interested in my epic fail...

The Falkland caracara's a majestic bird,
That few've ever seen (or much less heard)
So imagine my shock and utter dread,
When one day one landed on my head!

My son, he yelled and flapped in delight,
(He clearly did not share my paralysed fright)
And grumbled he was both disappointed and sad,
That this was an experience he'd not yet had

I heard his words and jumped into action-
Beckoned the falconer, who, in a fraction
Had the bird poised upon my dear child,
I soon saw the issue with a plaything so wild....

The flesh that the falconer used as a lure
Was the very same colour as my little son's ear!
And so being hungry, the beast took a nip
(Not his whole ear, mind you, just the tip)

And so, instead of something nice,
I'd made my child a sacrifice-
A tasty snack for a great big bird,
Talk about fail. I felt like a turd!

Life's full of crazy moments, you gotta go slow
Difficult experiences can be chances to grow,
Have you ever fed a loved one to a wild beast?
C'mon that's worth a few chuckles at least?!

Ever had a well-intentioned parenting moment blow up in your face? I could probably write a book about mine! Hah!

PLEASE promise you'll write to me if you too have ever accidentally fed your kid to a wild beast? I'm thinking of starting a support group…

Mad or Scared?

Somctimes the angriest parents
Are the ones who are most afraid,
(It's easier to hide the scars, you see
And this game is globally played)

'Tis the same part of one's brain after all
That's involved with both anger and fear,
And somehow one seems less embarrassing to show,
(That's why anger's more apt to appear):

A poor school system, an unfair grade,
An inattentive referee, whilst the game's being played
An undiscovered talent (that a scout just never found)
Or a painful situation witnessed on the playground...

The tricky thing about parent anger
Are the bridges that can get burned-
And most all of us have had moments
Where we wished we'd previously learned-

That when big feelings of anger
Come knocking on our door
It doesn't hurt to sometimes stop,
And mindfully implore
Our thinking to return to
This question that I love:
'What is it in this situation now,
That I'm most AFRAID of?'

Driving Fears Away

Dear reader I've something to confess:
I'm petrified to drive,
My palms get sweaty, my heart's a-thump
terrified I won't arrive,
At the place I'm trying to get to,
(in a single unharmed piece)
And the idea of driving a precious child,
is unthinkable to say the least!

See I frequently get real mixed up
with which way is left and right,
(Though I know on an intellectual level,
this idea I have to fight).
And today I had to face up
to this terrible demon inside,
See it was raining, pouring and storming-
behind excuses I could not hide

When my sweet little daughter looked at me
and said 'Mama you can do it I bet,
Drive me to that appointment,
we don't need to walk, it's yucky and wet!'
I took a deep breath and nodded,
I could not trust my voice,
I'd been preaching growth mindset to my kids,
now I didn't have a choice!

But to take a dose of my own medicine,
and finally do this task,
(Though I'd happily have preferred
just about any other ask!)
I'd driven the car just half of the way,
the sky was getting dark,
And then I remembered with horror
that I'd have to parallel park!

Taking deep breaths I steadied myself
(my kid was watching me)
This was a defining moment,
what kind of mum would she now see?
We got to the street,'twas jam packed,
no parking spot in sight,
(And here I needed space for two,
so I could 'slide' in right)

I closed my eyes, heaved a sigh,
and desperately started to pray,
And suddenly... just up ahead
a large SUV moved away!
It was nothing short of a miracle,
for from my spot across
The road I manoeuvered smoothly,
and parked like a total boss!

I'm still shaking as I write this,
though I now feel strangely free,
And all because my sweet little kid
showed such belief in me!

Have you ever tried to do something that was difficult for you, just for the sake of your kid(s)? In what ways have you become a better person since you became a parent?

LETTING GO

The Dirt on Hurt

Your kid's gonna get hurt
And eat a whole lotta dirt,
Just wait till they discover electrical sockets!!
There's no way to stop the pain,
and the experience they'll gain
Regardless of those Band-Aids in your pockets.

Parenting's a risky endeavour:
Baffles both feeble and clever,
Your heart is roaming freely outside your body
This business is just all-too-real,
Vicarious pain we REALLY feel,
Not to be attempted as a socially-sanctioned hobby!

But lest this scares you off,
or makes the cynics scoff
I must also present a balanced view-
This task you're undertaking,
Will consume your every waking,
But in the end, you'll emerge a wiser you.

Just don't confuse YOUR OWN fear,
With the reality of your dear
Kid's journey through the ups and downs of life,
For they only learn to 'rise'
By falling lots, and then....SURPRISE!
Your kid'll be equipped to deal with strife!

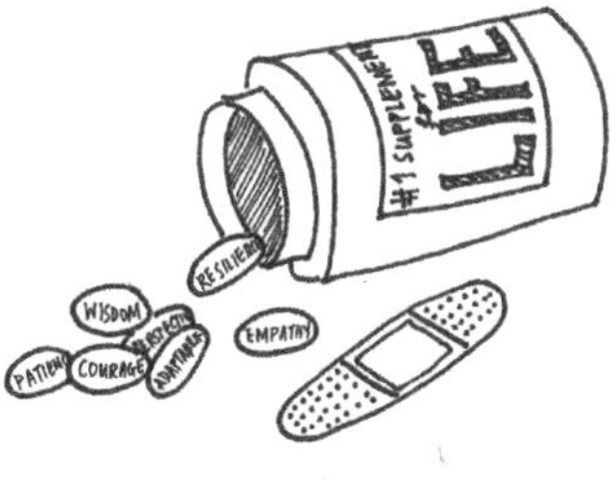

Octo-Parents

Octopus-mum, that's what she be!
Rushing around, not a second free-
Setting up play dates, doctor's visits and drives,
It's a miracle some days Octo-mum survives!

Coming round the corner, look- It's Octo-dad,
Wrangling baby plus groceries on the limited sleep he's had
Managing work appointments and make-up piano classes,
Looking for sports equipment, homework and lost glasses...

Octopus parents all wish for more hours,
A few extra limbs and time-bending superpowers
There's always something urgent that needs getting done,
So poor Octo-parents often miss out on fun.

The humble Sloth parent has a lesson to teach us,
Slow and relaxed, good-humoured Sloth reaches
A limit after which no rushing is done,
'Cos Sloth parent knows 'perfection' cannot be won!

Sloth parent gave up juggling, "Some ball's gotta fall,
My Sloth kids will survive it, they're like me- after all,
Life is just too short to go whizzing about,
Struggling with stress, being crippled with self-doubt."

Sloth kids, as a result, are both chilled and relaxed,
Sure they do fewer things, this is a fact-
But I heard the other day that sloths tend to live longer,
Maybe 'less is more' might make our kids stronger?

Equal Division of Labour

Think equal labour's just a nice-to have dream?
When parenting feels like a one-person team?
Here's a perspective worth its weight in gold:
Some parenting stories deserve to get old!

Both parents need alone time with baby,
As the principal caregiver sometimes,
To build confidence, competence and maybe
Manage a clear up after Poonami* crimes

The 'investment' made in these baby days,
Pays dividends more ways than one thinks:
Early bonding builds connection in powerful ways,
Along with skills, like cleaning bottoms in sinks

By challenging old norms too small for our wear
Neither parent will feel shortchanged or bored!
Our kids will see work distribution that's fair
And the economic potential can't be ignored!

**Poonami = a tsunami of poo.*

Disclaimer: This principle also holds true for families with same-sex couples and/or stay-at-home dads. Everyone wins with more equal division of parenting labour.

Each of us brings a 'little special something' - skills, viewpoints and solutions - to this parenting journey. How can we best ensure that our kids benefit from this?

Obedience: Holy Grail or Personality Fail?

Does one REALLY want obedient offspring?
Growing up where I did, it sure was a thing!

Quiet, docile, compliant kids
were very much in vogue,
For tongues would wag about those ones
who went a little rogue....
(Parents lived in terror that
their kids would bring down shame,
And do something terrible to
tarnish the family name)

The awful part of this charade
was truly that it did,
Hamper the freedom to connect
properly with one's own kid!
For sure, it's easy to manage
lots of day-to-day things,
When one doesn't have to navigate
huge tantrumy mood swings...

OK, I know, these kids sound
like an exhausted parent's dream,
Pssst..they're fictitious:
real kids DO (at times) scream;
It seems we might be wired for it,
surely disobedience has a place?
For after all, it's left its mark
across the history of our race...

I wonder if our ideas on this
Might be a wee bit muddled,
For a kid who's 'conditioned obedient'
will surely be befuddled,
When faced with situations where
the rules and one's values clash,
Are we truly preparing our dear kids
for the realities of real life's trash?

That boss who thinks the rules are made
simply to be bent?
(The one who spends more money than
can actually be spent)
Or how about the bully who forces
your kids' head under water,
Feeding off the insecurities of
your dear son or darling daughter?

Perhaps that tiny bit of spunk
(that might come across 'disobedient')
Is a crucial part of an important
self-preserving ingredient?
Perhaps instead of celebrating
compliance that is blind
We ought to raise our kids to be
respectful and independent of mind?

The way we communicate with our kids,
our act of parenting,
Is more crucial now than ever before-
It's emotional investing!
'Connection before correction'
as that famous maxim goes,
Instead of 'obedience'- affection,
respect and regard that grows!

For the values we espouse,
the communication that we shape,
Are our very real-world legacies,
That tomorrow's adults will ape;
And our world needs more free thinkers,
unafraid of breaking the rules,
(Especially those created by
dictatorial or bigoted fools)

How can we best teach our kids the value of civil disobedience in situations when their rights or the rights of others are being affected? How can we ensure that they understand the importance of moderation and non-violent means of expressing their beliefs?

The Highly-Sensitive Child

The highly-sensitive child,
Might take a little while,
To adjust to, (some moments can be tough)
It might be a loud noise,
Or particular kinds of toys,
Or a carpet or clothing that's too rough...

Other days a lack of sleep,
Is that thing that will keep,
You as a parent, teetering on the brink-
If you've a highly-sensitive child,
You know the ride can be wild,
(And you're petrified of what others think!)

Then there are other days,
When your child acts in ways,
That makes you wonder: "Was it all a bad dream?
This sensitive child,
Is SO loving and mild,
Look at us, we're an absolute dream team!"

Fellow parent, remember THESE days,
Because your child won't always,
Be around with something you're expected to 'fix'-
For in time they too will grow,
As you and I both know,
Every phase brings a new, exciting mix:
Of abilities and skills,
And the battle of wills,
That you're surely engaging with your kid,
Will prepare them in some way,
For that bright future day,
when they self-advocate because of all you did!

HUMOR
PEACE
TIME
HOPE
JOY
FORGIVENESS
LOVE

Raising Agents

Raising kids starts with us raising ourselves-
Can we manage those triggers when our little 'house elves'
Get up to all mischief, push all of our knobs
Delaying appointments, up-ending our jobs?

How the sweet heck's this supposed to all work?
Can we feel empathy when we feel like the jerk-
Who just wants to scream- "bloody hell, I've had it, you know..."?
(Paradoxically these moments present chances to grow)

It won't always work- we're bound to mess up-
But here's a little thought that might fill your cup:

Either we manage, to re-establish connection
In the midst of the chaos, (with gentle redirection)

Or we just 'lose it'... if this happens, don't despair-
Move on, after rupture, you STILL can repair...

We owe it to our kids to show them 'humanness' too
None of us are infallible, we're ALL creatures who
Thrive on connection, respect and self-worth:
And EVERYONE is worthy, from the moment of birth.

(We might need to unlearn some things we've been taught-
Definitely some narratives we unwillingly 'bought')

'Cause when the ADULTS change, then everything changes
The behaviour we might seek is right within our own ranges...
We are mirrors or prisms, we radiate and reflect-
(This bit's a truth that's more comfortable to deflect...)

How do I know this? Oh the struggle is true-
I battle my demons daily - is that how it is for you?

MORE RACE
MORE RACE
MORE ACE
MORE GRACE
STILL MORE GRACE
MORE GRACE

Space for Grace

When we give our kids grace,
They learn to freely embrace
The wonders that they hold within
The world's crazy rat race,
Won't pin them in place
And we won't feel paralysed by sin-

For the act of given grace,
Creates an especial place
That helps both giver and receiver grow-
So let's mindfully give grace,
For the survival of our race
It matters far more than we'll ever know!

When we give our kids grace,
They learn to love their own face
Knowing that the welcome is guaranteed,
And that act of giving grace,
Empowers them to take up space
And ask for help whenever they're in need

So when we ponder on this task,
Of parenting, we must ask
Is there really a whole lot we need to know?
The answer my dear friend,
Is devastatingly simple in the end
It's grace that will help both them and us grow!

Grace/giving grace in this context is about showing kindness to our kids even when we think they don't deserve it. This can be by going out of our way to show compassion, kindness and love to them in difficult times, even if they might not appreciate it or recognise it. This rhyme is specially dedicated to parents raising teenagers in their 'prickly' phase.

Kid Views on the News

Sometimes I hear things on the news,
I know I'm not to hear,
(Mom or dad switch off the TV,
when they notice that I'm near.)

I think it's 'cause the grownups
are making a right mess of things,
And they don't want us kids to know
how badly it all stinks!

But sometimes I cannot help it,
Like when Bob or Billie Sue,
Talk about things they've heard somewhere,
And I wonder if it's true...

Some of the stories make me angry,
Like the ones where animals are killed,
It makes me wonder what the big 'uns are doing-
Aren't grown-ups supposed to be skilled?

Then there are stories of wars breaking out,
In countries both far and near,
I hear of tanks, people leaving their homes,
This part makes me feel fear.

There are stories of things that make you sick,
So we have to stay in and do school,
In our homes with our parents as teachers,
(This can sometimes be sooooo uncool!)

And every so often I hear a bit,
Too awful to even repeat,
(These are the stories that make mum and dad,
Nervously stare at their feet)

I sometimes think in my little mind,
That they feel very much like me,
That's why they try to keep this stuff in,
They want my thoughts to be free!

But sometimes it just doesn't work at all
The bad news is just too big,
I hear half-stories that make no sense
(So for details I have to dig!)

I know my parents really love me,
They're always doing their best,
But sometimes I get the feeling,
That they really just need a rest,
From the horrible awful stories,
We hear on the news each day,
And so my friends and I have decided,
To do things a different way!

So watch out world, we're coming,
And in just a few short years,
We'll change how things run on this planet,
So OUR world will cry far fewer tears!

We know you cannot help it,
(After all we're smarter than you,)
We'll pay attention to DIFFERENT things
When we build our world anew!

Sincerely,
THE KIDS

Parent tip: It's a helpful idea to first find out what one's kid(s) knows about a certain distressing news event before attempting to offer any (developmentally appropriate) explanations.

Can I trust this? Fake or real?: As our kids get older, regular, open discussions about the importance of critical evaluation of 'news' sources is important. This applies to wide-ranging topics such as playground gossip, relationship rumours, online images, marketing and news/video sources. The big question is…how will we get better at this as adults so we can guide them in the way they deserve?

Updates

'This too, will pass, it's just a phase'
Words that you'll hear oft repeated,
Those early days crawl by (in a sleep deprived haze)
As aspects of your kid get 'deleted'.

Replaced instead with a newer 'version',
Little one's trying out novel tricks,
Suddenly mobile, with a big 'no' aversion,
Reality hits – (It's a ton of Lego bricks)

Like an automatic mobile phone update
Development is a double edged blade:
Just figured things out? Time's up, too late!
Here's the next challenge, lest you get staid!

Thing is, each phase has beautiful parts
That we mourn the loss of when gone,
Earlier versions of our kids, etched into our hearts
Exist no more on this side of the pond.

This journey is a string of hellos and goodbyes,
They're rapidly changing (as we are, my friend)
We must learn to see things with present-focused eyes,
For we'll not walk this way again.

Mini Me...or Not

My youngest kid struggles with school,
And his social skills ain't that hot-
I'm cracking my brain
(sometimes quite in vain)
For truly there's not much I've not
Tried in the name of support, intervention,
Something to lighten his load,
I'm a parent with the best of intentions,
I just want to smoothen his road!

I know I'm not alone in my struggles,
Everyone has something or other,
But why does MY kid inspire pitying looks,
(Whilst others hero-worship his brother?)

I love both my kids equally,
Trust me, truly I do,
But one has his stuff all in order,
And the other has simply no clue!

So I feel that the expression of my love,
Has to take a slightly different form-
For the one is independent and able,
(The other defies the concept of 'norm')

I wonder if my genes are to blame,
Especially because what I see,
Are more than my hair colour and features,
This kid's a younger version of me!

And I so desperately want to know he'll survive,
(I remember tough times in my past,)
To find people who'll accept him and help him
to thrive
And not pick him for sports teams the last...

Someone who'll help in moments he dreads,
And a trusty watch guard for a prank,
Someone patient when he's forgotten his meds,
(Just a true friend for him to be frank!)

Although when I look at him clearly,
There's something much more that I see,
This kid whom I love so dearly,
Has strengths that were never part of me!

Perhaps his journey will be different than mine,
He's got far more support than I had,
Who knows, he may turn out better than fine,
(This thought makes me feel rather glad!)

Maybe, just maybe I need to amend,
This mind-prison I've personally built,
And trust that all will be fine in the end,
To hell with my parenting guilt!

The job he's destined to have one day,
Has probably not been invented yet,
I'll advocate and support as he makes his OWN way,
That's it, my mind is all set!

Dedicated to the many, many parents who have voiced this inner journey to me throughout the years. Our kids will find their way eventually... Our job is to advocate for them, love them fiercely and support them in being the individuals that they are. They are NOT mini versions of us, no matter how often we hear things that might suggest otherwise.

COMMUNICATION

Professional Development for CEOs

Have sticky little hands thrown in a wrench?
Those best laid plans now give off a stench?
One look around you- WHOOOOOSH! in
they barge,
(Did they miss the memo that YOU'RE the
one in charge?)

Out in the 'real world' you're a CEO,
Your calls are held immediately whenever
you say so,
Employees hang expectantly on the
instructions that you say,
Comfortably a black and white world
(with little to no grey).

Then along comes a critter who changes up
these things,
Has you questioning your sanity as she
gleefully runs rings,
Around everything you knew up till then to
be true-
When managing crises and people...
(negotiations too).

Known to bring industry leaders crashing to
their knees,
They'll make you re-examine goals (not to
mention priorities)
Prepared for radical unlearning? Then you
may just well find,
Parenting is professional development of the
very finest kind!

Teen Speak

I say 'up',
You hear 'down',
I'm trying to be funny
I only see you frown.

I think that I'm quite savvy
You're thinking KPC*
It's like I need a GPS
For the chasm 'tween you and me

I sorely want to hear
'Bout what's going on inside
(Whilst crippled by unknown fear
On this bumpy, soul-stretching ride)

Where's the baby I remember?
The toddler I tickled for hours?
In his place: an uber-cool member;
With stoic ignoring powers.

I long for the old connection,
Though I know, this too, will pass-
I always thought we'd be the exception
(That I'd not need THIS parenting class...)

But this lesson, seems I too, must learn,
You're your own independent being:
I was once where you are, now's your turn
And I desperately want you to feel seen!

Will we ever speak the same speak?
For a brief moment, perhaps, in between
(When you're older and feeling weak
'Cos you're parenting YOUR OWN teen)

And then, the moment will pass
We might need translation again-
For with advancing years, alas!
I'll speak the language of the aging brain.

Translation:
KPC = keeping parents clueless

Dedicated to all parents out there currently wrestling with the all-too-real generational communication gaps between parents and teens.

How can we best show our love, when words just don't seem enough?

Manual NOT Automatic

Relationships are KEY
They are not automatically a 'given'
Grown with time and consistency,
And countless shortcomings forgiven.

Our kids don't owe us allegiance:
This must be fought for and EARNED-
And ignoring this 'inconvenience'
Has been known to get parents burned!

Yeasterday

Today I sat with my kid,
as we watched some baking bread rise,
As it expanded in the oven,
I watched her sharp, alert eyes,
'What makes it go so fluffy, Mama?
How does it actually start?'
(So I explained the important science,
of how sugar makes yeast fart)

And then I got to thinking
about how our words are like sugar too,
Kind utterances can be such wonderful lifts,
When others are feeling blue!
And so I thought I'd share some of mine,
with you my much-loved tribe,
So if you feel you need a lift
I invite you to imbibe:

And share some uplifting feedback
with another person you hold dear,
Let's see if this circle of care
can become one gigantic sphere
And if you're looking for inspiration
I can truly tell you it's wise,
To watch for everyday wonders
through the lens of childhood's eyes.

Surface Listening

'Surface listening' is really easy-
we humans do it all of the time!
Nodding our heads, pretending we've heard
(Whilst miles away in our minds…)

As a kid I was certainly very adept,
At listening in this particular 'style',
With a neutral expression I totally kept
Teachers thinking "What an attentive child…"

I may have heard the sounds that were made
Might even have managed to respond
I knew this was important to get a good grade,
But of this farce I was certainly not fond!

As a kid I remember thinking
"No one really hears what I say
One day when I'm a grown up
I hope I don't act in this way!"

"Listen closely, no more questions!"
we were so often told
"Pay attention and be quiet, so
you'll know things when you're old."

But no one ever told us,
that to really do this part,
Listening with ears is not enough,
one must listen with one's heart!

And age has nothing to do with it,
A deep listener can also be young,
Anyone can listen to really understand
(The rest is just cow dung!)

Sometimes I catch myself ‘surface listening’
With the intention of responding fast,
I want the complainer to just go away
Alas this ‘listening’ is just a farce.

Are you listening to respond?
Or is it understanding that you seek?
Are you listening to memorise facts
Cos you’re secretly a bit of a geek?

We must watch ourselves, ‘tis too easy
To lapse into ‘adults know best’
But our kids are watching our listening
We can’t afford to fail this test!

Who listened to you best when you were a child? What do you think your kid would say in answer to this question?

THIS IS...
THE WAY
#My Way or the Highway

This is the Way

Kids do as we do,
And not as we say-
They're not Mandalorians,
So "This is the way"
Is not going to change
How they behave or they think
And if you force your ideas
They'll kick up a stink!

Formalising Normalising

We are normalising behaviours with our actions every day,
Every family builds its own 'normal' with things we do or say
Ok, none of us are really 'normal'- I hear you, truly I do,
But there are certain ways we behave, that actively shapes our crew:

The way we speak, our choice of words, mannerisms, even our tone;
The way we gravitate like zombies towards our beloved mobile phone,
The way we might laugh and joke/or treat a family member,
Some things can get so hardwired, that we barely even remember

A time when these habits might've looked a different way
But dear parent, do take heart, there's always time today
To take a moment to be mindful, 'bout ONE thing you wish to start
Normalising within your family (start with the head, lead with the heart)

For the act of recognition that "it's always been this way"
Is a lie we tell ourselves that permits habits which shouldn't stay:
So look deeply at some aspect of YOUR own family life
What behaviour isn't serving you and causing family strife?

And if this feels too big to carry, and it's courage that you seek,
Remember this little hack, for when you're feeling weak:
Think about your parenting wins, about the things you're doing right
This will help you realise, you've got all you need for this fight!

My Son, BE the Sun!

THE WORLD DOESN'T REVOLVE AROUND YOU
(though to me, you are the bright sun)
This lesson you must learn while you're new
Or it will cost you moments of fun:

The brightest of those in our sphere
Shine their light, so OTHERS feel warm
A powerful way to combat that fear
And navigate many a storm

So be the sun to others,
Light is needed everywhere!
Though the world doesn't revolve around you
You've got something only YOU can share.

'No' is a Word of Love

'No' is a word of love
That we sometimes don't use enough
When our kids are so small
(cute dimply cheeks and all)
Saying 'no' can sometimes be tough!

Saying no can be a tiring thing:
Might our beloved child chuck a fit?
What will others think
if we're pushed to the brink-
of the point where we lose our s#!t?

But 'no' is a powerful word
It helps important messages be heard-
And must be taught in young years,
To prevent bigger tears,
Lest it become a thing that's feared.

Saying 'no' doesn't make us unkind-
It's not a form of rejection,
Depersonalising 'no'
Is the way to go:
'It's not YOU I'm rejecting, it's your action'

As parents we must be clear:
'no' occupies a distinct place-
It is not to be mean,
Belittle or demean,
Or a means to control any space

Dear parent, oh please don't wait
To teach this love word to your kid
There'll be moments of strife,
At all points in their life,
And you'll be ever-so-thankful you did!

We all need to take 'no' with some grace
As we go about things day-to-day
And accepting the word 'no'
Is a life-skill we must grow,
And practice helps in a VERY big way!

What are some things that can help us say 'no' to our kids when it is needed? How can we get better at recognising these moments?

How might we balance the 'no's with the 'yes'-es on important things that align with our values and our kids' needs?

Parent Speak

"We communicate in totally different ways,
How's this partnership supposed to function?
When consistent messaging between us strays,
And snags at many a junction..."

Resentment can build when one parent
Feels like they're stuck always 'the bad guy',
Whilst the other one thinks "Life's too short to be strict-
What if disaster strikes and we die?"

I've seen this before - a thousand times more -
We all have our own 'parent speak';
But to weather this road (and what lies in store)
A common language we must really seek.

Personality, experience all shape our speech,
Whether responding or supporting our critters,
Furthermore us adults- we're not easy to teach:
But it's possible if we are not quitters!

We're all rewriting the narratives we learned,
About what parenting should ideally 'look like'-
We might carry baggage, perhaps many times burned
Our demons yelling 'Go take a damn hike!'

We need to adjust shared expectations and speak,
As we pursue some kind of balanced middle road,
Consistency is the thing that most kids seek,
(And a parent who doesn't inappropriately 'unload')

The elephant in the room of course-
Is to do this we must GROW UP ourselves
And who knows? It might just save one divorce
If we're brave enough to deeply delve?

COMMUNITY COURAGE

Parents Anonymous

Managing this steep parenting climb
(Especially when doing it for the first time)
Is not without its challenges and bumps,
Every new parent needs a friend,
Navigating a similar bend,
Like sleepless nights and hair falling out in clumps!

It's important for one's sanity,
To know that this profanity,
That's become one's life is simply not unique-
So for one's mental health,
One needs the especial wealth,
Of a buddy who is ALSO up S#!t Creek!

The shared moments of commiseration
(or indeed sheer desperation)
Seem less painful when one's not suffering alone-
For a buddy with a baby
Is a lifeline... and just maybe,
Readily accessible talk therapy by phone!

Did you get a bunch of unsolicited, well-intentioned, but crazy bits of advice as a new parent? What support did you yearn for most in those early days? Has this changed from the kind of support you would wish for now?

Judgement Daze

"OMG did you hear what she fed her kid?
Sugar cookies, ice cream and s'mores!!"

"But did you hear what that crazy dad did?
He forces his kids to do real house chores!!"

"And what about that snobby mum,
Who's too stuck up for a play date?"

"Do you know that chaotic, frazzled, jogpant nut,
Who's just ditsy, unprepared, always late?"

"Have you seen how they keep their house??
It's so disgusting I'd never go in!"

By the judgements we dish out thoughtlessly,
None of us would be without sin!

There's no right way to be a parent,
We're all improvising as we go along,
Our hopes and fears (not apparent),
Battling demons that tell us we're wrong...

So whenever a judgy feeling
starts swelling up in our chest,
We must be sure to squash it-
(Most of us are trying our best!)

Instead let's celebrate fellow mums and dads
We all need supportive community
Disclaimer: Except in the case of actual abuse,
then judge/report with impunity!

Crooked Crowns

Wordlessly fix those lipstick smears,
Straighten that crooked crown!
Help a fellow parent back onto their feet
Lend a hand, when they've fallen down…
Watch mindfully for the time to use words,
Silence is sometimes the best
No parent is spared, we've ALL felt like turds
And suffered the odd sanity test-
But each and every one of us needs
Support from a tribe on this road:
For in those moments our wounded heart bleeds
It helps to be able to unload
In a place where judgment isn't feared:
The ear of someone who cares
None of us is immune, (cos that would be weird),
It's just a thing that not everyone shares.

Choices

"A natural birth (with no drugs)
is Mother Nature 's own way!
Those poor C-section babies,
they just don't have a say
About when they are ready
to emerge onto this plain,
How can their mums be so thoughtless-
are they just scared of pain?"

"Everyone knows
breast milk is the best-
Those Formula parents
just failed their first test,
Sure it's convenient,
but it's got less vitamins-
Don't these folks want
a baby who wins?"

"Co-sleeping is crucial
for healthy connection,
Parents who value attachment
show their affection,
By sharing their bed
with their newest little one!"
(Who's got time for any other bedroom fun?)

"What do you mean
you're going back to your job?
You don't need the money,
why be a career snob?
You're letting someone else
raise your little one?
You'll be missing out
on once-in-a-lifetime fun!"

Choices, so many choices
on this tricky parenting road!
And lots of wonky opinions
(uninvited by the crapload),

Whatever one decides,
there is bound to be someone,
A know-it-all who 'means the best',
but makes you want to run!

But as we ride upon
this rollercoaster-choice-terrain,
This 'keep-it-real' advice is best
Held close to one's heart and brain:

Choices are made within context:
Everyone's reality's diverse-
And by honouring decisions made in this way,
One puts one's own family first!

And choosing NOT to have any kids,
is something to be honoured too,
Everyone's journey is different,
no one needs the pressure to prove,
Anything to another person,
however 'correct' the picture may seem-
For we're all living our own screwy lives,
not someone else's Insta-dream!

What choices are you proudest of making
as a parent?

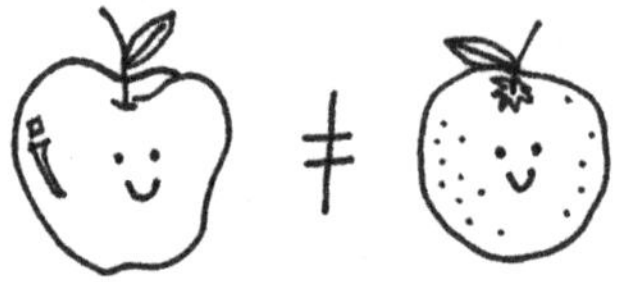

Comparison

Everyone's baby is different,
Comparison's a parenting trap,
And bragging about all your baby can do-
Is a douche move (no one gives a crap!)

Instead what every new parent needs:
The cheerleading voice of a friend,
Who reminds "Great trees grow from teeny
tiny seeds,
baby'll crawl, walk, talk in the end!"

So take heart if your baby is moving,
At a pace that's completely their own,
It's not a race, it's not about proving
Your kid's winning on 'Milestone Throne'

We can choose to sidestep this pressure
If we are smart when we choose our words,
No one's journey is 'made to measure'
And comparison is for the turds!

BEING A
GOOD ENOUGH
PARENT
TRAUMA

Trauma

Trauma can take many different forms-
Unexpectedly surfacing within our life's storms
Personal trauma, generational pain,
Wounds that're inflicted over and over again:
Whole nations face trauma; they stare aghast
At repeating bloody patterns within their own past-

When will we learn, we're interconnected, ONE race
Whose only hope of surviving this space,
Rests in being able to look on above,
Seeing our fellow humans with respect and with love?

Imagine what would happen in a world where we
Made teaching THIS point our priority:
Might the generations to come endure less pain
Of the prejudicial cancer of the untravelled brain?

Most all of us have been victims in some way, shape or form. How can we ensure that this is not a future norm?

Families are Weird

Families are truly weird-
'Normal' doesn't statistically exist,
Forget those stories you might've heard,
There's always some quirky ol' twist:

That seemingly innocuous 'normal bunch'
Living behind that white picket fence?
They're crazy and unique (no one has a hunch
They've mastered distraction/pretence)

What about that perfect-looking troop,
With their immaculately manicured lawn?
Oh trust me, they are one REAL weird group,
You don't see, cos their curtains are drawn!

We've been conditioned to think that weird = strange,
A pathology to fix, conceal or to change-
With fictitious 'normal' infesting our think,
Many a parent's been brought to the brink...

But people ARE weird,
So this I ask you
Why wouldn't this apply
To any family crew?

Trust me, as a therapist, I tell you no lies,
These illusions of 'normal' are one great disguise,
Cos 'normal' looks different to both me and to you-
So how can it be conceptually meaningful too?

The next time you think that your family is weird,
Embrace it and celebrate, for haven't you heard?
There's no one else like you, you glorious freak,
You do you as you are, if self-acceptance you seek!

Ode to the Unsung Heroes...

There's a tribe of unsung heroes,
in every place you look-
You'll find them in every country,
every corner, every nook
They are tenacious and resilient,
because they've had to be,
The deep power that lives
inside of them, simply amazes me.

Do you know who I'm talking about?
Have you got a clue?
Yes, dear single parent,
I'm talking about YOU!
You do this job day in day out,
some days it's impossibly tough,
At times you struggle to be kind to yourself
you can be rather rough-

You might wrestle with the pressure
of how things 'ought to be,'
Deep down inside you might wonder
what it's like to be really free
Of the voices in your head that shout
'You really missed that mark,'
Or simply have someone to share
your worries after dark.

For some, to parent on one's own
has had a healing effect on the past,
I celebrate you, as you reclaim that throne-
you've reshaped the die that was cast
The reasons that you walk this road,
in a solitary state,
Are varied and deeply complicated,
a twist or chosen fate

Yet somehow you get out there
in the role of both mum and dad,
In your mission to be the best caregiver
your kid has ever had!
YOU are enormously bigger
than your status of singlehood,
Your hopes and dreams, they matter
As everybody's should!

And so today I challenge you
to find a way to take,
This chance to celebrate yourself
(plus a tiny little break!)

And remember these words of wisdom
for the times when things get tough,
You've come this far, you're worthy,
Dear parent YOU are enough.

Finish Line

Congratulations, my fellow parent,
You've made it to the very last page,
I hope you've felt understood and seen
And now realise YOU'RE wise as a sage-
Knowing that the most important tools
And answers within YOU does lurk,
For the cleverest of men and the greatest of fools
Don't succeed this without serious self-work!